How to use this book 

Follow the advice, in italics, where given.

Support the children as they read the text that is shaded in cream.

Praise *the children at every step!*

Detailed guidance is provided in the Read Write Inc. Phonics Handbook.

Activity 8 (Answer the 'questions to read and answer') only appears in Sets 4–7.

8 reading activities

Children:

1 *Practise reading the speed sounds.*
2 *Read the green and red words for the non-fiction text.*
3 *Listen as you read the introduction.*
4 *Discuss the vocabulary check with you.*
5 *Read the non-fiction text.*
6 *Re-read the non-fiction text and discuss the 'questions to talk about'.*
7 *Re-read the non-fiction text with fluency and expression.*
9 *Practise reading the speed words.*

Speed sounds

Consonants *Say the pure sounds (do not add 'uh').*

f	l ll	m	n	r	s ss	v (ve)	z s	(sh)	th	(ng) (nk)

b	c k ck	d dd	g gg	h	j	p (pp)	qu	t tt	w wh	x	y	ch tch

Vowels *Say the vowel sound and then the word, e.g. 'a', 'at'.*

at	hen	in	on	up	day	see	high	blow	zoo

*Each box contains one sound but sometimes more than one grapheme. Focus graphemes are **circled**.*

Green words

shop   fish   fresh   from   tank   pick

much   add   drop   just   with

gra` vel ➔ gravel

plant ➔ plants   shop ➔ shopping

the do you water too*

food* cold* goldfish*

red for this book only

A pet goldfish

Introduction

Have you got any pets?
Have you ever looked after pet fish?
Do you know what you have to do to
care for a pet? In this book you will
learn how to look after a pet goldfish.

Written by Gill Munton

Vocabulary check

Discuss the meaning (as used in the non-fiction text) after the children have read the word.

	definition
gravel	*tiny bits of stone*
water plants	*plants that live and grow under water*

Punctuation to note:

You Put	
	Capital letters that start sentences
.	*Full stop at the end of each sentence*
!	*Exclamation mark*
–	*A dash to show that more information follows*
,	*Comma to show a pause*

You can get a goldfish from
a pet shop.

Shopping list

- a **goldfish**
- a tank
- gravel
- **water** plants
- fish **food**
- a net

1. Put gravel in the tank.

2. Add water plants.

3. Add fresh water
– not too hot and
not too cold.

4. Tip the fish in.

5. Drop fish food in the tank – just a bit, not too much.

Do not pick the fish up!
Catch it with a net.

Questions to talk about 

Re-read the page. Read the question to the children. Tell them whether it is a FIND IT question or PROVE IT question.

FIND IT	**PROVE IT**
✓ *Turn to the page* ✓ *Read the question* ✓ *Find the answer*	✓ *Turn to the page* ✓ *Read the question* ✓ *Find your evidence* ✓ *Explain why*

Page 9:	FIND IT	*Where can you buy goldfish?*
Page 11:	FIND IT	*What should you put in the tank first?*
Page 13:	PROVE IT	*Why do you think the water must be the right temperature?*
Page 15:	FIND IT	*How much food should you put into the tank?*
Page 16:	FIND IT	*What mustn't you do?*

Speed words

Children practise reading the words across the rows, down the columns and in and out of order clearly and quickly.

shop	from	pick	drop	tank
add	fish	much	with	pet
put	just	gravel	not	fresh
net	catch	tip	plant	hot